# EP
# Geography and Cultures
# Printables:
# Levels 1-4

This book belongs to:

_____

This book was made for your convenience. It is available for printing from the Easy Peasy All-in-One Homeschool website. It contains all of the printables from Easy Peasy's geography and cultures course. The instructions for each page are found in the online course.

Easy Peasy All-in-One Homeschool is a free online homeschool curriculum providing high quality education for children around the globe. It provides complete courses for preschool through high school graduation. For EP's curriculum visit allinonehomeschool.com.

## EP Geography and Cultures Printables: Levels 1-4

ISBN: 9798566557618

First Edition: December 2020

# Map Keys

Practice with map keys. North (N) goes at the top of the compass rose. South (S) is at the bottom. East (E) is at the right. West (W) is at the left. You are going to look at the pictures and see if they are up (N), to the right (E), etc. What do the pictures mean? Can you read the map key?

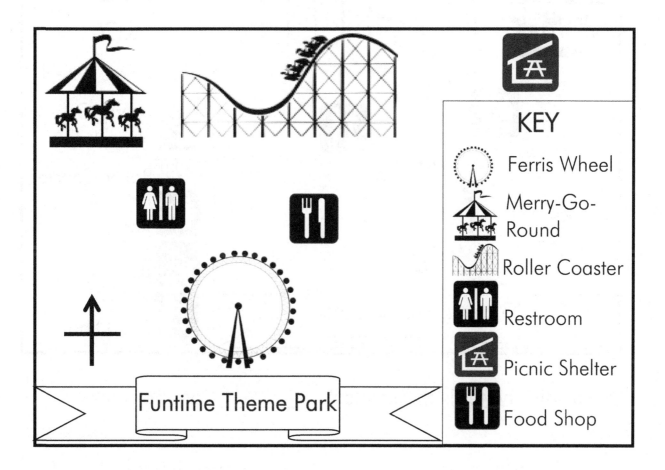

# Map Keys

Label the compass rose with N, S, E, and W. Then answer the questions below the map using the words north, south, east, or west.

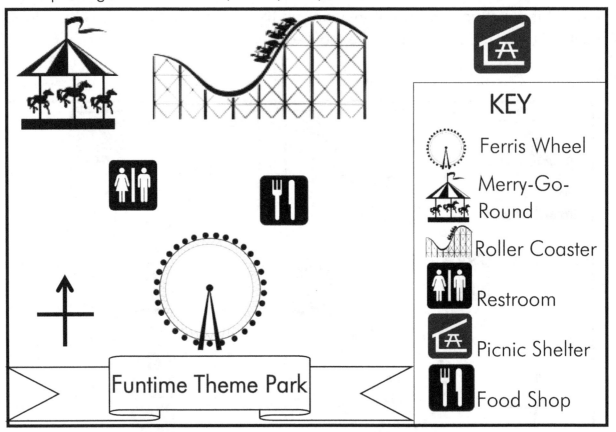

The picnic shelter is the farthest _____ on the map.

The roller coaster is _____ of the ferris wheel.

The restroom is _____ of the food shop.

The ferris wheel is the farthest _____ on the map.

The merry-go-round is _____ of the roller coaster.

# Floor Plan

Label the floor plan below according to the directions on the next page. Draw a compass rose if you want help with your directions.

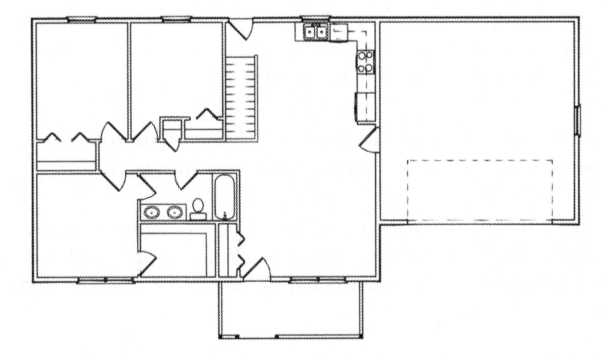

The southern-most part of the house is the front porch. Label it FRONT PORCH and draw a plant on it. South of the front porch there is a path leading away from the house. Draw it.

Going north from the front porch, you enter a large room. The southern half of the room is the living room. Label it LIVING ROOM and add a sofa. The northern half of the room is the kitchen. Label it KITCHEN. Draw a pot on the stove.

The northwestern-most room in the home is the guest bedroom. Label it GUEST BEDROOM and draw a bed in the room. (In the southern part of the guest bedroom there is a small closet.)

Directly east of the guest bedroom is the library. This room is to the west of the kitchen. Label it LIBRARY and draw some books in it.

The room to the south of the guest bedroom is the master bedroom. Label it MASTER BEDROOM. Draw a bed in this room. East of this room there is a bathroom and a large closet. Label the CLOSET and draw a shirt in it.

The largest room of the floor plan is the garage. This family has turned it into a GAME ROOM. Label it and draw what you would want in your game room.

Heading north out the kitchen door is the BACKYARD. Label it and draw a tree in it.

## Passport

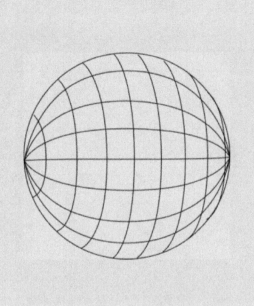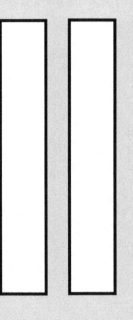

**PASSPORT**

(This page left intentionally blank)

Country: _____

Picture of flag:

Name: _____

Nationality: _____

Gender: _____

Date of birth: _____

Date of issue: _____

Date of expiration: _____

Picture

Signature: _____

(This page left intentionally blank)

Countries visited:

Countries visited:

(This page left intentionally blank)

Countries visited:

Countries visited:

(This page left intentionally blank)

# United Kingdom

Using the map linked online, label each country of the UK on this map: England, Wales, Scotland, and Northern Ireland. Color each country a different color. Label each capital: London, England; Cardiff, Wales; Edinburgh, Scotland; Belfast, Northern Ireland.

https://d-maps.com/carte.php?num_car=5542&lang=en

# World Map

3000 km (equat.)

2000 mi (equat.)

© d-maps.com

# All About England

| Famous person/people from this country: | A famous landmark (write or draw): |
|---|---|
|  |  |

| | |
|---|---|
| Capital City | |
| Population | |
| Climate | |
| Languages Spoken | |
| Bordering Countries | |

Other fun facts about the country:

# All About France

| Famous person/people from this country: | A famous landmark (write or draw): |
|---|---|
|  |  |

| | |
|---|---|
| Capital City |  |
| Population |  |
| Climate |  |
| Languages Spoken |  |
| Bordering Countries |  |

Other fun facts about the country:

# Europe

Label what you can of this map. You can simply point and verbally name the countries if you'd like. Do you remember any capitals?

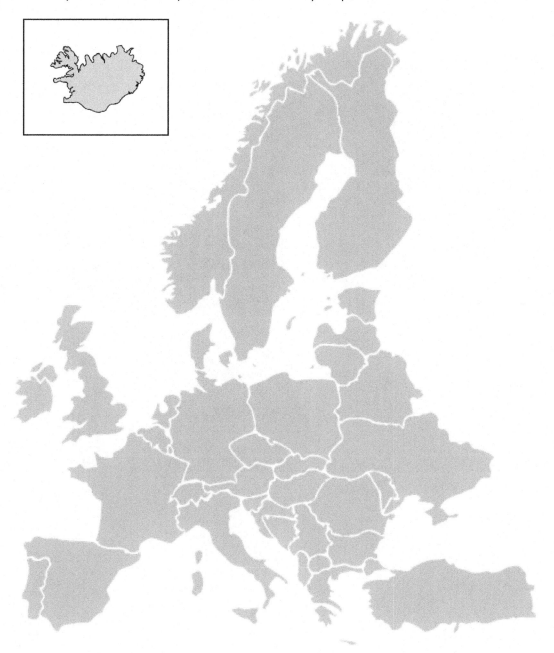

# Africa

Follow the directions in the online course to label the map.

# All About South Africa

| Famous person/people from this country: | A famous landmark (write or draw): |
|---|---|
| | |

| | |
|---|---|
| Capital City | |
| Population | |
| Climate | |
| Languages Spoken | |
| Bordering Countries | |

Other fun facts about the country:

(This page left intentionally blank)

# Kenya Lapbook

Cut out the rectangle and fold in on the dotted line. Read the information about ugali. Label the front of your folded piece.

| | How to make ugali: |
|---|---|
| Ugali is served and eaten daily with dinner. | Mix 1 cup yellow cornmeal with 4 cups of water. Bring to a boil. Stir and mush continually until it pulls away from the sides of the pan without sticking. Cover the pan and let it stand. |

Cut out the hexagons and stack in order: flag, black, red, green, shield. Staple them together. Color the red and green parts of the flag using the image in the online course to guide you. Read the information about the Kenyan flag and tell someone something you learned.

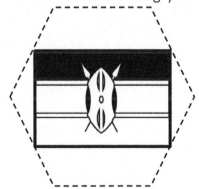

Black represents the African people.

Red denotes the blood that was shed in their fight for freedom.

Green symbolizes their rich natural resources.

The shield and spears signify their readiness to defend their land.

(This page left intentionally blank)

# Kenya Lapbook

Cut out the rectangle as one piece. Fold the left side in (on the line at **A**), and fold the right side in (on the line at **B**). Cut on the dotted lines so you have four strips you can open to the fold. The strips will be your cover and you'll lift each strip to reveal the answer.

More than 31 million people

Mountains, savannah, jungles, beaches, deserts

Swahili, English, tribal languages

Kenyan shillings - $1 ≈ 80 shillings

↑ A

(glue here)

↓ B

How many people live in Kenya?

What is the Kenyan landscape like?

What languages are spoken in Kenya?

What type of money is used in Kenya?

(This page left intentionally blank)

# Kenya Lapbook

Cut each piece out in full (don't cut off the tab label). The piece without the tab is the cover. Stack them in order – cover, Capital, Continent, Lakes, Ocean – and staple.

## All About Kenya

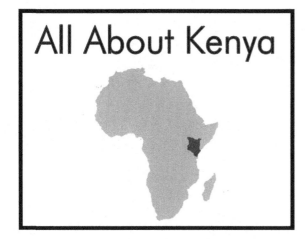

## Nairobi is the capital of Kenya.

Capital

## Kenya is part of the continent of Africa.

Continent

(This page left intentionally blank)

Lake Victoria and Lake Turkana are Kenya's biggest lakes.

Lakes

Kenya borders the Indian Ocean.

Ocean

(This page left intentionally blank)

## Kenya Lapbook

Cut around the outside of the first circle, as well as along the dotted lines to cut out the "cut out here" section. Cut around the outside of the second circle. Stack the first circle on the second circle and secure with a brad. Spin the top wheel to read about the animals of Kenya.

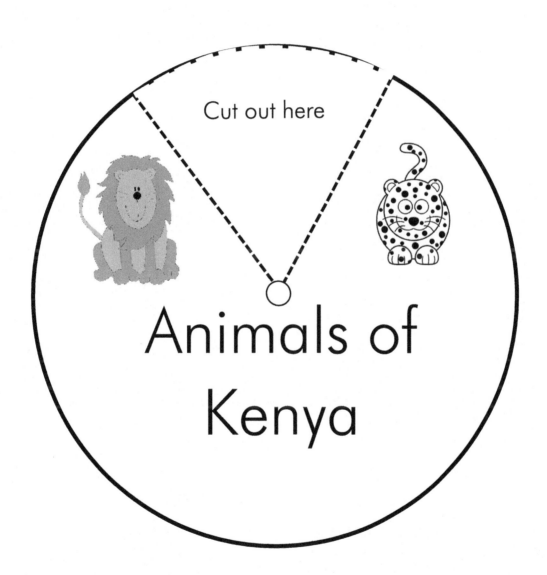

Cut out here

Animals of Kenya

(This page left intentionally blank)

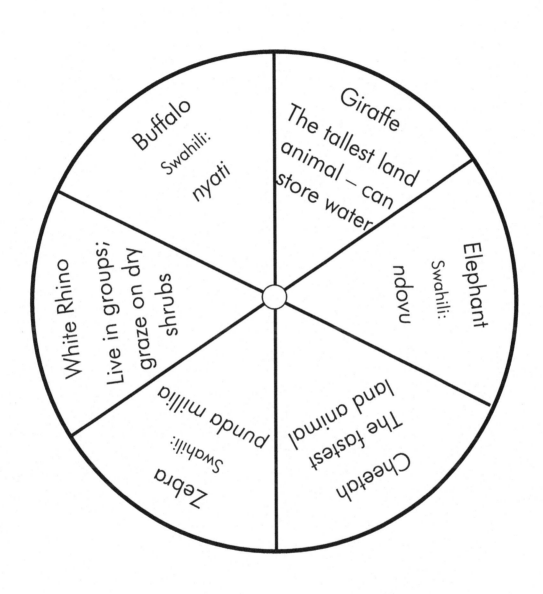

Giraffe
The tallest land animal – can store water

Elephant
Swahili:
ndovu

Cheetah
The fastest land animal

Zebra
Swahili:
punda millia

White Rhino
Live in groups; graze on dry shrubs

Buffalo
Swahili:
nyati

(This page left intentionally blank)

# All About Nigeria

| Famous person/people from this country: | A famous landmark (write or draw): |
|---|---|
|  |  |

| | |
|---|---|
| Capital City |  |
| Population |  |
| Climate |  |
| Languages Spoken |  |
| Bordering Countries |  |

Other fun facts about the country:

# Nigerian Flag

Color the Nigerian flag and read about its history.

The current flag of Nigeria was chosen in 1959 from a redesign contest. It is made up of two outer green bands, representing the fertile land of Nigeria, and a middle white band that represents peace and unity.

Nigeria celebrated its independence from Britain on October 1, 1960. The Union Jack was lowered, and the new Nigerian flag was raised for the first time.

# James Cook

Use this page to write some facts about James Cook.

_____

_____

_____

_____

_____

_____

# Australia

Draw the deserts and the mountains of Australia on this map.

# Eastern Hemisphere

Show someone else how much you know about this map. Tell them about the oceans, continents, and whatever countries you can.

adapted from:   https://d-maps.com/carte.php?num_car=13181&lang=en

# Asia

Use this map as you begin to learn the countries of Asia in the online course.
Show which countries were not included in your lesson.

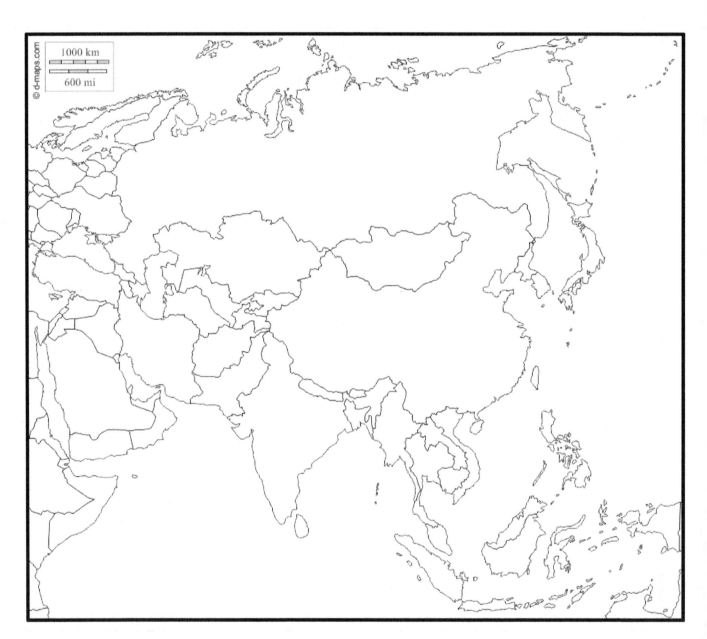

# Middle East

Color each country a different color. Use the map in the online course to help you.

(This page left intentionally blank)

# Turkey Lapbook

Cut out as one piece. Fold down the middle to cover the words and crease the fold. Cut along each dotted line. Close all the flaps and on each one write the English word that matches the Turkish word. (In order: bread, cheese, tea, rice, soup, milk, apple.)

| | |
|---|---|
| ekmek  (ek-**mek**) | |
| peynir  (**pay-near**) | |
| çay  (**chigh**) | |
| pirinç  (peer-**eench**) | |
| çorba  (**chore**-bah) | |
| süt  ("**suit**") | |
| elma  (el-**mah**) | |

(This page left intentionally blank)

## Turkey Lapbook

Cut out the two pieces. Glue the Turkey rectangle into the blank space of the frame. Continue to the next page.

(This page left intentionally blank)

# Turkey Lapbook

Cut out map. Glue or tape onto the back of the frame from the previous page. Cut out the information rectangle. Staple it behind the frame on the left side so the frame opens like a book to reveal the map and information. (Please note the lira conversion is always changing and may be significantly different from what's printed!)

Turkey is a large and ancient country. Some say even part of the Garden of Eden was located there. In fact several parts of the Bible can be mapped in Turkey, including Mount Ararat where Noah's ark landed.

Turkey is a "bridge" from Europe to Asia. The city of Istanbul is divided by water and part of the city stands on each continent.

Turkey has always been a desirable country because it is surrounded on many sides by water. It has a long history of being invaded. Turkey became a Muslim nation when the Ottomans attacked and took control in 1299.

The language in Turkey is called Turkish. Their money is called the Turkish Lira. One lira is about 65 cents. This is their new money. They recently changed from their old system where one dollar equaled more than one million lira!

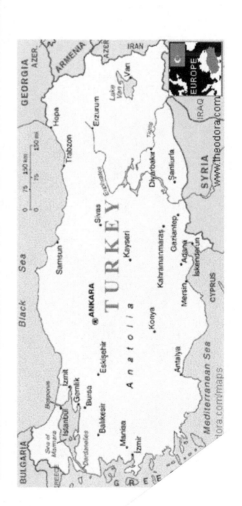

(This page left intentionally blank)

# Turkey Lapbook

Cut out each of the four rectangles (this page and the next). Write the answers to the questions inside the folded pieces.

What city in Turkey lies in both Asia and Europe?

What's the capital of Turkey?

(This page left intentionally blank)

# Turkey Lapbook

Where in Turkey did Noah's ark land?

Which three seas surround Turkey?

(This page left intentionally blank)

## Turkey Lapbook

Cut out each mealtime rectangle. Arrange all six mealtime rectangles in order with the smallest on top. Staple them together.

# Mealtime in Turkey

Bread
Salami
Olives
Jam
Honey
Tea
Feta cheese

What's for breakfast?

(This page left intentionally blank)

Lentil soup

What's for lunch?

Green beans
Rice (cooked
with vermicelli)
Cucumbers
(topped with mint)

What's for dinner?

(This page left intentionally blank)

## Lentil Soup

One onion
One carrot, grated
One cup red lentils
Tomato paste
Salt

Chop onion. Cook in a tablespoon of oil for a few minutes. Add a tablespoon of tomato paste. Continue to stir for a couple minutes. Pour in six cups of water. Add red lentils and grated carrot. Cover and boil over low heat about an hour. Salt to taste.

RECIPES

## Green Beans

Two onions
Three tomatoes
One pound of beans cut into 1-inch pieces
Two heads of garlic
One third cup olive oil
One teaspoon both salt and sugar

Slice onion and tomato thinly. Cover bottom of pan with beans. Spread onion and tomato slices on top of beans. Add chopped garlic. Pour over oil and 1/3 cup hot water. Sprinkle over salt and sugar. Cover and boil over low heat for about an hour.

(This page left intentionally blank)

# Turkey Lapbook

Cut out the x and the other circles. Stack them with the x on top, "Extreme Temperatures" next. Staple in the corner. On the next page, cut the two circles. On the bottom circle, cut out the wedge along the thick black line. Place that circle on top of the other circle and fasten to each other with a brad.

Extreme
Temperatures

Turkey is a large
country so there are
very hot spots and
very cold spots.

The
hottest and
coldest recorded
temperatures in
Turkey are
119° F and
-49° F.

(This page left intentionally blank)

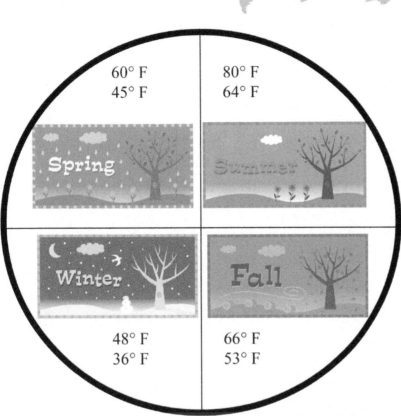

60° F
45° F

80° F
64° F

48° F
36° F

66° F
53° F

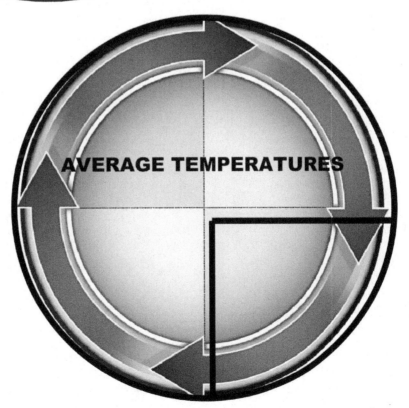

Geography/Cultures
Levels 1-4

(This page left intentionally blank)

# Turkey Lapbook

Cut out these five pictures from Istanbul. Include the captions and try to make them all the same size. Put your favorite picture on top and staple them along the top.

*Simit* **for sale!**

**"Evil eye" jewelry is said to protect you from evil.**

(This page left intentionally blank)

**The second oldest metro in the world is in Istanbul.**

**Mosques can be seen all along Istanbul's skyline.**

**People take boats like buses to get around Istanbul.**

(This page left intentionally blank)

# Russian Flag

Color the Russian flag and read about its history.

The Russian flag has three equal horizontal stripes colored white on top, blue in the middle, and red on the bottom. This design was first used by Peter the Great, and it was used from 1883 until 1917 and the Bolshevik revolution. When the communist regime fell in 1991, the flag was reinstated as the official Russian flag.

# All About Russia

| Famous person/people from this country: | A famous landmark (write or draw): |
|---|---|
| | |

| | |
|---|---|
| Capital City | |
| Population | |
| Climate | |
| Languages Spoken | |
| Bordering Countries | |

Other fun facts about the country:

## Inuit Lapbook

Cut each piece out in full (don't cut off the tab label). Write information on each piece from the online page. Stack the pieces in the order they appear here and staple.

# Inuit Life

-AN ESKIMO KITCHEN NOME ALASKA-

## What kind of homes did they live in?

homes

Geography/Cultures
Levels 1-4

(This page left intentionally blank)

What was their clothing like?

clothing

What did they eat?

food

(This page left intentionally blank)

What other interesting
facts did you learn?

other

(This page left intentionally blank)

# Inuit Lapbook

Cut the piece out in full and fold on the dotted line. Write facts about Inuit arts and crafts inside.

(glue here)

# Inuit
# Arts and Crafts

(This page left intentionally blank)

# Inuit Lapbook

Cut the piece out in full and fold on the dotted line. Write facts about Inuksuit inside.

## Inuksuit

(This page left intentionally blank)

# Inuit Lapbook

Cut the big rectangle as one piece and fold the outside squares in on the line so they close over the middle. Glue the label pieces on top of the folded piece. On the inside, write facts about summer in the Arctic.

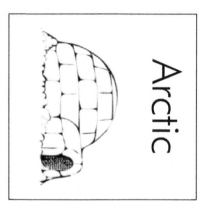

Arctic

Summer

(This page left intentionally blank)

# Inuit Lapbook

Cut out the hexagons and stack them with the cover piece on top. Write some facts about Inuit games on the blank hexagons. Staple and add to your lapbook.

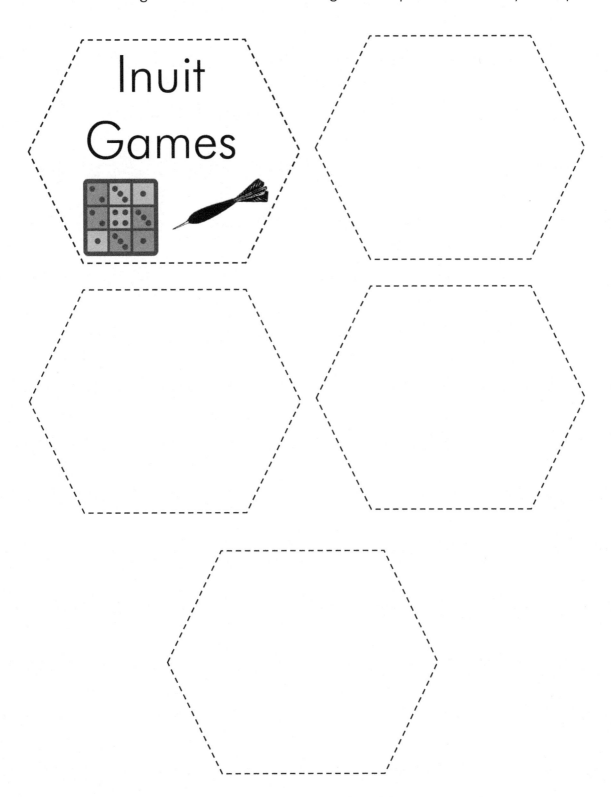

(This page left intentionally blank)

# South America

Use this map of South America along with the online lessons.

1000 km

600 mi

© d-maps.com

https://d-maps.com/carte.php?num_car=2312&lang=en

# Brazilian Flag

Color the flag of Brazil using the flag in the online course as a guide.

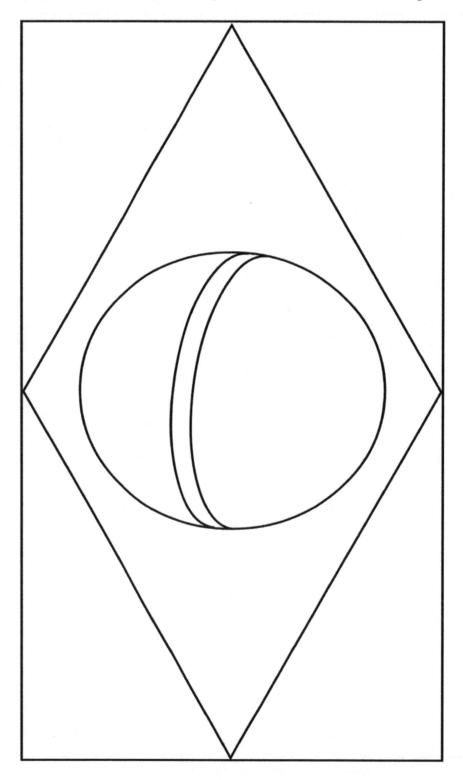

# Brazil Lapbook

Cut out each picture with its description as one piece (you should have three total pieces). Stack them in this order: "Rio de Janeiro" on top, "Christ the Redeemer" in the middle, "Carnaval" on the bottom. Staple at the top.

"Rio" is the second-largest city in Brazil.

## Rio de Janeiro

This famous statue is a symbol of the Catholic country. It's on top of a mountain, 2,400 feet above the city.

## Christ the Redeemer

This is a dancer at the festival held four days before Ash Wednesday each year.

## Carnaval

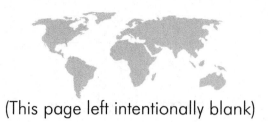

(This page left intentionally blank)

# Brazil Lapbook

Color in Brazil, the largest country in South America, and then color the only two countries that do not touch Brazil's border. Using the same colors, color in the map key so the color you used on the map matches the color next to the country's name. Use an atlas, globe or the internet to find out the country names. Cut out along rectangle.

KEY

☐ Brazil

☐ Chile

☐ Ecuador

https://d-maps.com/carte.php?num_car=2312&lang=en

(This page left intentionally blank)

# Brazil Lapbook

Cut out as one piece. Fold in the right-hand side first so the words are on the inside. Crease the fold. Then cut along the dotted lines. On the other side of each flap you can copy the word written on it. For example, on the back of the "Money" flap, write "Money." Fold in left side so that the Portuguese words are on the inside. The blank side on top is the cover.

| Capital | Population | Size | Language | Money |
|---|---|---|---|---|
| Brasilia | 190 Million | about 3,280,000 sq. miles | Portuguese | Real |

Learn Portuguese!

Te amo!
Chee-**ah**-moe
"I love you!"

Você me ama?
**Voe**-say-mee-**ah**-mah
"Do you love me?"

Geography/Cultures
Levels 1-4

(This page left intentionally blank)

# Brazil Lapbook

Color in each section of the pie chart whatever color you like. Color in the labels to match the chart. For example the largest part of the pie chart should match the largest number in the label (51%). Whatever color you use to color in the smallest section of the chart, you should use to color in the label for the smallest number, 5%.

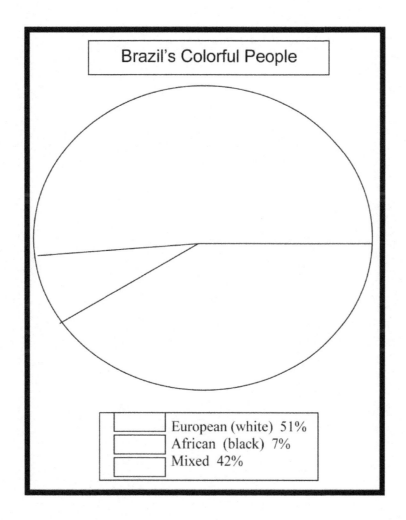

Brazil's Colorful People

European (white) 51%
African (black) 7%
Mixed 42%

(This page left intentionally blank)

# Brazil Lapbook

Cut out as one big piece. Fold accordion style so that the words are on the inside and the picture is the cover. Crease well. Attach to lapbook by gluing down the back of "Soccer is…"

Soccer is Brazil's favorite sport and one of the world's most famous players ever, Pelé, was Brazilian.

In Brazil, as in much of the world, soccer is called a version of the word "football." Doesn't that make a lot of sense?

(This page left intentionally blank)

# Brazil Lapbook

Cut out the boxes as one piece. Fold down the middle so the words are on the outside. Inside write the answer: New Year's Eve. Attach it to the lapbook. Cut out the ovals as one piece. Fold down the middle so that the question is on the cover. Open and write the answer on the inside. It's WINTER!

On what day
does everyone
wear white?

Which season
starts in June?

(This page left intentionally blank)

# Brazil Lapbook

Cut out picture and "deforestation" rectangle. Staple them together at the top with the picture as the cover and the words on the inside. Attach to lapbook. Cut out "Amazon" as a long rectangle or oval and attach to lapbook.

**Deforestation** is the cutting down of trees in a forest. The most trees are cut down in the Amazon jungle because people want the land for farming. In the last few years about 5,000 square miles of trees were cut down each year.

(This page left intentionally blank)

# Brazil Lapbook

Cut out as one piece. Attach to cover of booklet on next page.

Geography/Cultures
Levels 1-4

(This page left intentionally blank)

# Brazil Lapbook

Cut out as one piece. Fold down the middle so the words are on the inside. Glue the animal pictures to the cover. Then cut between each picture so you have three mini books. Attach to lapbook gluing or taping the backside of the words.

The Green Anaconda is the largest snake in the world.  It can grow to 29 feet long!

The Spider Monkey can use its tail to grip tightly to a branch.

Macaws can live to be 50 years old or sometimes even older.

(This page left intentionally blank)

# Brazil Lapbook

Cut out these two strips each as one piece. Fold down the top so the words are on the inside. Don't worry about the bottom not lining up. Attach to lapbook. Color the cover: the top half of the strip (river) should be a light sandy brown, the bottom half of the strip (river) should be a dark muddy brown.

**teem**: to be full of things; The Amazon River is teeming with life means that there are many things living in it, like piranhas!

The Amazon River is the second longest river in the world, but it dumps more water into the ocean than any other river. It has more than one thousand branches to it and is **teeming** with life. Some parts of the river are light colored and some are dark because of the ground where the rivers form. When a "white" branch of the river meets a "black" branch of the river, the two colors run side by side for miles before mixing together.

(This page left intentionally blank)

# Argentine Flag

Color the flag of Argentina and read about its history.

The Argentine flag has three equal horizontal stripes colored light blue on top and bottom and white in the middle. The center of the white band contains a golden sun known as the "Sun of May" which was based on the design of the first Argentine coin. This flag was first flown in 1812 during the War for Independence from Spain. It was adopted as the national flag in 1816, and the "Sun of May" was added in 1818.

# All About Argentina

| Famous person/people from this country: | A famous landmark (write or draw): |
|---|---|
| | |

| | |
|---|---|
| Capital City | |
| Population | |
| Climate | |
| Languages Spoken | |
| Bordering Countries | |

Other fun facts about the country:

# Central America

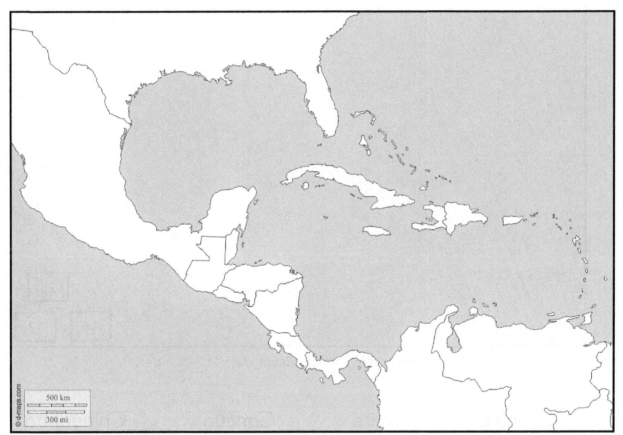

https://d-maps.com/carte.php?num_car=1388&lang=en

# Mexico

Fill in the blanks below with the number from the map. The plain numbers are cities. The boxed numbers are countries.

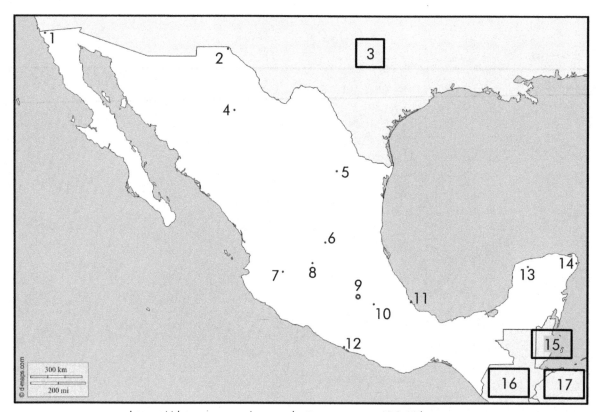

https://d-maps.com/carte.php?num_car=4124&lang=en

___Acapulco    ___Belize    ___Cancun    ___Chihuahua

___Juarez    ___Guadalajara    ___Guatemala    ___Honduras

___Leon    ___Merida    ___Mexico City    ___Monterrey

___Puebla    ___San Luis Potosi    ___Tijuana

___United States    ___Veracruz

# North America

1000 km

600 mi

© d-maps.com

https://d-maps.com/carte.php?num_car=1404&lang=en

# Mexican Flag

Color the flag of Mexico and read about its history.

The Mexican flag has three equal horizontal stripes colored green, white, and red from left to right. The center of the white band contains a coat of arms with an eagle perched on a cactus and holding a serpent. Aztec legend tells the tale of a nomadic leader having a dream of coming across an eagle perched on a cactus eating a snake. They were to build a city there. The city is now Mexico City. This flag wasn't officially adopted until 1968, though it's been around since 1821.

# All About Mexico

| Famous person/people from this country: | A famous landmark (write or draw): |
|---|---|
|  |  |

| | |
|---|---|
| Capital City | |
| Population | |
| Climate | |
| Languages Spoken | |
| Bordering Countries | |

Other fun facts about the country:

# The Mountain States

Label each state and write its abbreviation. Use the US map to help you.

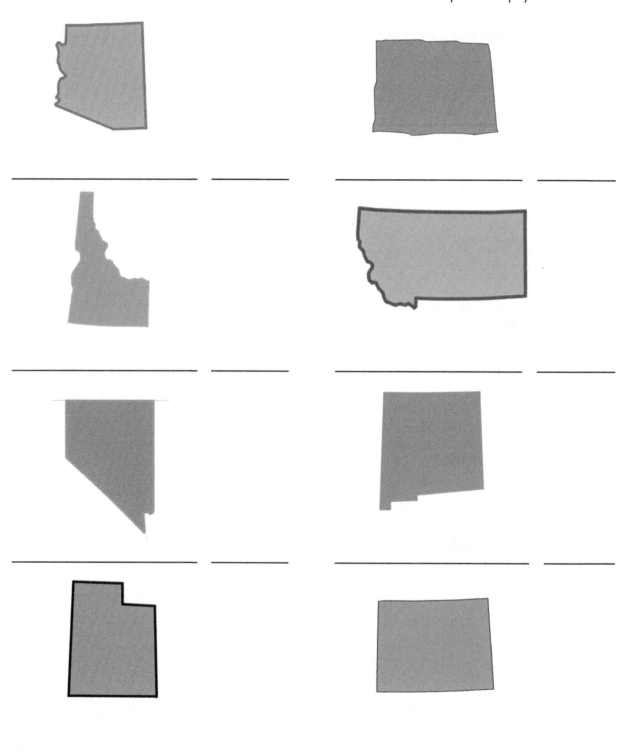

# United States of America

Use this map to learn the postal abbreviations of the US states.

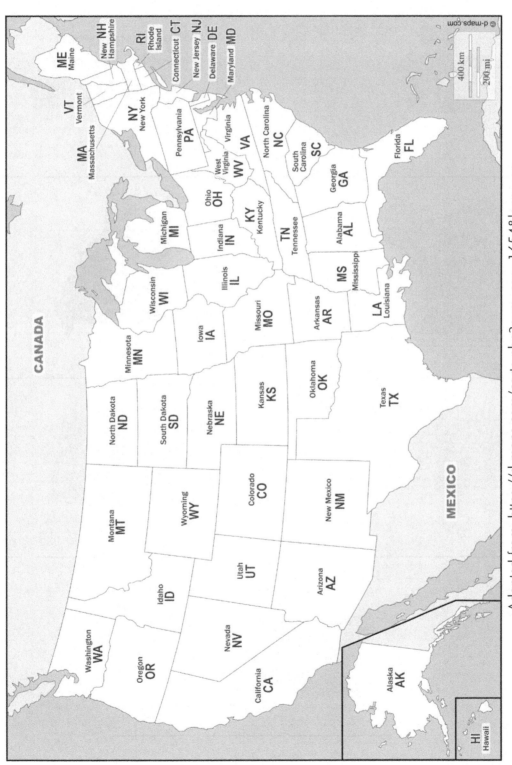

Adapted from: https://d-maps.com/carte.php?num_car=1654&lang=en

# West North Central States

Label each state and write its abbreviation. Use the US map to help you.

_____  _____          _____  _____

_____  _____          _____  _____

_____  _____          _____  _____

_____  _____

# Pacific States

Label each state and write its abbreviation. Use the US map to help you.

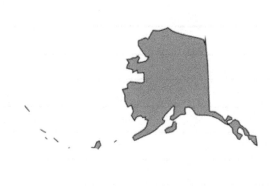     

_____  _____      _____  _____

_____  _____      _____  _____

_____  _____

# United States Flag

Color the flag of the United States and read about its history.

The flag of the United States of America, nicknamed "The Stars and Stripes" or "Old Glory," has thirteen stripes, symbolizing the thirteen original colonies. Seven of the stripes are red, signifying the blood that was shed for independence, and six of the stripes are white, standing for purity and innocence. There are 50 white stars, representing the 50 current states. They are on a field of blue, standing for perseverance and justice.

# New England States

Label each state and write its abbreviation. Use the US map to help you.

_____  _____

_____  _____

_____  _____

_____  _____

_____  _____

_____  _____

(This page left intentionally blank)

# United States Landmarks

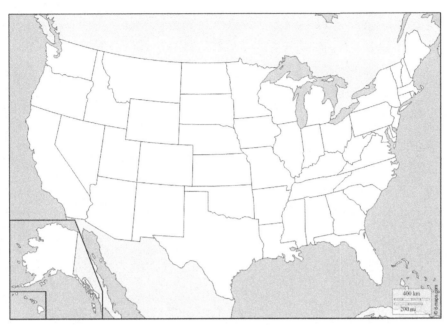

https://d-maps.com/carte.php?num_car=1652&lang=en

The Washington Monument, located in Washington, D.C., is a tribute to George Washington.

(This page left intentionally blank)

The Lincoln Memorial is also in Washington, D.C., and honors Abraham Lincoln.

---

The White House, another landmark in Washington, D.C., is the home of the President of the United States.

(This page left intentionally blank)

Mount Rushmore honors four former presidents: George Washington, Thomas Jefferson, Abraham Lincoln, and Theodore Roosevelt. It is located in South Dakota.

The Gateway Arch, also known as the Gateway to the West, is located in St. Louis, Missouri.

(This page left intentionally blank)

The Statue of Liberty is a gift from France that stands in New York Harbor.

---

The Empire State Building is famous for having been the tallest building in New York City for so long.

(This page left intentionally blank)

Most famously rung upon the first public reading of the Declaration of Independence; the Liberty Bell is on display in Philadelphia, Pennsylvania.

The Alamo marks the site of a famous battle. It is located in San Antonio, Texas.

(This page left intentionally blank)

The Space Needle in Seattle, Washington, was built for the 1962 World's Fair.

The Golden Gate Bridge (which is actually red), crosses San Francisco Bay in California.

(This page left intentionally blank)

# United States of America

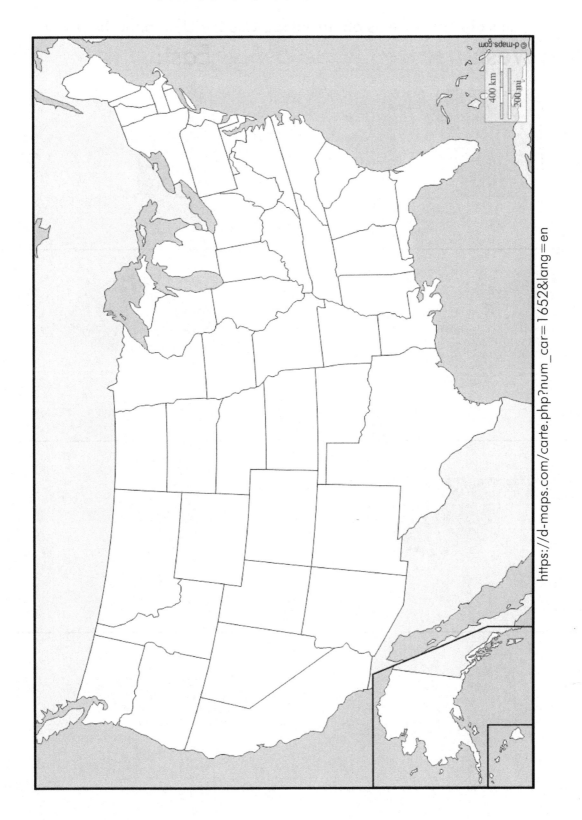

400 km

200 mi

© d-maps.com

# South Central States

Label each state and write its abbreviation. Use the US map to help you.

## West:

## East:

_____  _____    _____  _____

_____  _____    _____  _____

_____  _____    _____  _____

_____  _____    _____  _____

# East North Central States

Label each state and write its abbreviation. Use the US map to help you.

_____   _____      _____   _____


_____   _____      _____   _____


_____   _____

# South Atlantic States

Label each state and write its abbreviation. Use the US map to help you.

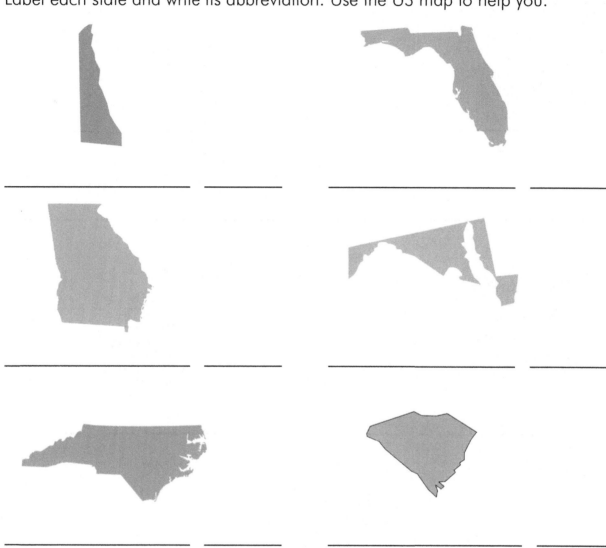

_____  _____

_____  _____

_____  _____

_____  _____

# Middle Atlantic States

Label each state and write its abbreviation. Use the US map to help you.

_____ _____

_____ _____

_____ _____

# Postal Abbreviations

Circle the letters in the state name that make up its postal abbreviation (given for you). The first one is done for you. Most states form their abbreviation from their first two letters or their first and last letter. Two-word states use the first letter of each word. Put a check mark beside the nine states that don't follow this norm.

| | | | | |
|---|---|---|---|---|
| AL | (A)labama | MT | Montana |
| AK | Alaska | NE | Nebraska |
| AZ | Arizona | NV | Nevada |
| AR | Arkansas | NH | New Hampshire |
| CA | California | NJ | New Jersey |
| CO | Colorado | NM | New Mexico |
| CT | Connecticut | NY | New York |
| DE | Delaware | NC | North Carolina |
| FL | Florida | ND | North Dakota |
| GA | Georgia | OH | Ohio |
| HI | Hawaii | OK | Oklahoma |
| ID | Idaho | OR | Oregon |
| IL | Illinois | PA | Pennsylvania |
| IN | Indiana | RI | Rhode Island |
| IA | Iowa | SC | South Carolina |
| KS | Kansas | SD | South Dakota |
| KY | Kentucky | TN | Tennessee |
| LA | Louisiana | TX | Texas |
| ME | Maine | UT | Utah |
| MD | Maryland | VT | Vermont |
| MA | Massachussetts | VA | Virginia |
| MI | Michigan | WA | Washington |
| MN | Minnesota | WV | West Virginia |
| MS | Mississippi | WI | Wisconsin |
| MO | Missouri | WY | Wyoming |

# Postal Abbreviations

Draw a line to match the state name to its abbreviation.

| | | | |
|---|---|---|---|
| AR | Alabama | NE | Montana |
| CA | Alaska | NH | Nebraska |
| AL | Arizona | NJ | Nevada |
| AK | Arkansas | MT | New Hampshire |
| AZ | California | NV | New Jersey |
| | | | |
| CT | Colorado | NY | New Mexico |
| FL | Connecticut | ND | New York |
| GA | Delaware | OH | North Carolina |
| CO | Florida | NM | North Dakota |
| DE | Georgia | NC | Ohio |
| | | | |
| ID | Hawaii | OR | Oklahoma |
| IA | Idaho | RI | Oregon |
| IL | Illinois | SC | Pennsylvania |
| HI | Indiana | OK | Rhode Island |
| IN | Iowa | PA | South Carolina |
| | | | |
| MD | Kansas | TX | South Dakota |
| ME | Kentucky | TN | Tennessee |
| KY | Louisiana | UT | Texas |
| LA | Maine | VT | Utah |
| KS | Maryland | SD | Vermont |
| | | | |
| MO | Massachussetts | WI | Virginia |
| MS | Michigan | VA | Washington |
| MI | Minnesota | WY | West Virginia |
| MN | Mississippi | WA | Wisconsin |
| MA | Missouri | WV | Wyoming |

# My City

Fill in these blanks about your city.

The name of my city: _____

My favorite restaurant in my city: _____

My favorite place to visit in my city: _____

The mayor of my city: _____

My city has a lot of: _____

# My State

Fill in these blanks about your state.

The name of my state: _____

The capital of my state: _____

My state bird: _____

My state tree: _____

The governor of my state: _____

| My state flag: | My state map: |
| --- | --- |
| | |

# My State Map

Draw a map of your state. Label it using the online link. Include a map key.

# All About My State: _____

Map:

Flag:

| | |
|---|---|
| State Number: | |
| Year Admitted: | |
| Capital: | |
| Region: | |
| Bordering States: | |

Bird:

Tree/Flower:

Made in the USA
Coppell, TX
13 September 2024

37095774R00079